FUSING GLASS HANDBOOK

A COMPLETE STEP BY STEP GUIDE ON FUSSING GLASS

GLENN ELLIS

Table of Contents

CHAPTER ONE

Fusing Glass

A Complete Guide

It's possible to make both useful objects and beautiful works of art by fusing glass. It is possible to learn how to safely cut and fuse glass into a single piece by doing glass fusing.

Glass fusing is a technique that you may not be familiar with.

When two sheets of glass are fused together in a kiln at approximately 1490 degrees Fahrenheit, the glass is fused.

Using this technique, you'll be able to create one-of-a-kind pieces of glass art. Glass fusing, unlike many other forms of glasswork, gives you as much time as you need to bring your designs to life.

Fused glass is a term used to describe a specific type of glass.

When two or more pieces of glass are heated in a kiln, the result is a single piece of fused glass.

Glass fusing is an art form.

Plates, tiles, bowls, jewelry, wall hangings, and other artistic creations are all made from fused glass. To make a finished piece of fused glass, all you need is a kiln and a few basic tools. Bulk production of vessels and other objects that are difficult or impossible to fabricate in a kiln uses glass blowing. Using a large furnace to melt the glass and a variety of other tools is necessary for glass blowing. Glass is cast in a mold, kiln-fired, and then coldworked with grinding and polishing equipment to create a three-dimensional sculpture. A torch is used in glass flameworking to create a finished object, but the process can only handle smaller items.

Before You Begin

Glass that is easily combustible

Choosing the right fusing glass is critical. The kiln must be able to handle the heat and cool without breaking the glass.

All your scraps from other projects won't be suitable for

fusing now, which is unfortunate.

For the fusion to be successful, all of the components must be compatible with one another.

Bullseye and Spectrum are the most popular manufacturers of what is referred to as "Fusible Glass." System 96 is the name given to Spectrum's fusing range.

How heated glass behaves

1/4 inch is the ideal thickness for fusing glass (6mm).

You can no longer get an exact square piece of 1/8 (3mm) sheetglass after firing it in a kiln.

In order to make the square more rounded and larger, fire three layers of 3/8inch/9mm glass.

Is there a second layer? Perfect. The glass retains its square shape and is the same size.

Needed Resources

An assortment of fusible glass, a pattern, a glass cutter and other cutting tools, as well as grozing pliers and other cleaning supplies, are all required.

A grinder is optional.

How to make glass fuse together

There is no limit to what you can create with fused glass once you have the proper equipment and studio safety in place. You can choose to fuse it flat or add texture, mixed media, and other elements. Slumped glass art is made by starting with a fusing process. To get started with fusing, here are the basic steps.

The first step is to set up your work area.

Gather the necessary materials and equipment for cutting glass. Use a kiln wash or firing paper to line the shelf of your kiln.

Step 2: Get your drink ready.

Shape the glass to your liking. However, if you'd prefer a smoother finish, you can always grind down the edges of your pieces. Ensure that the glass is free of smudges and fingerprints before using. Smudges can burn into glass and leave a mark if it is dirty when it is placed in the kiln.

Assembly of your glass is the third step.

Assemble the project in the kiln, being careful not to place it too close to the shelf edge or to other projects already there.

CHAPTER TWO

Glue a small amount of glass pieces together with a tacking technique when creating intricate designs. Even a small amount helps to keep your design intact when transporting your pieces into the kiln. A large amount will leave residue after firing.

- **Step 4: Light your work of art.**

Set the kiln's temperature and timers appropriately. Make sure the glass is completely cool before removing it from the kiln.

- **Step 5: Take a look at your work of art!**

Observe your stunning work of fusing glass! Slumping your fused glass requires inspecting the edges for any rough or sharp spots. Starting from the backside, use a grinder or diamond hand pad to smooth out any sharp edges before moving forward.

Glass slumping is an optional step in Step 6.

Make sure the piece is securely in place before firing to the desired slumping temperature. Aside from that, the piece is complete and ready to be displayed or put to use. Hand wash all fused glass and treat it delicately at all times.

This pattern was created by Daniel using a patterned bar flow fusing technique. For this project, the glass is placed in an oven where it is heated to the point where it melts together and forms a single piece.

She fused and slumped the glass to create patterns and depth in this work. The copper accents were also part of her design.

Getting started with glass fusing

There are numerous online resources, but the best way to learn is to attend a class in person. A glass fusing class under the direction of an expert glass artist is a must if you want to produce the best possible results. If you're just getting started, an in-person class will be less expensive than buying and setting up your own home glass fusing studio. Setting up your own studio is expensive, so it's best to start with an in-person class.

You can take classes at The Crucible where you will learn how to melt and shape glass in a kiln to make functional items like plates and bowls or art pieces of your own. Individual classes teach you how to combine colors, paint on glass, and use recycled materials to make beautiful art. There is no limit to what The Crucible can do for you when it comes to sculpting and melting glass. We offer a wide range of classes, from 3-Hour Tasters to more in-depth intensives like Glass Fusing and Slumping I, to give you a brief introduction to the art of glass fusing. A self-guided Glass Fusing and Slumping Lab is another option after you've got the basics down.

FAQs about glass fusing

What type of glass should I use for fusing glass?

Fusing soda-lime glass is common because of the wide temperature range of the kiln and the wide variety of accessory glass that can be used for design purposes. Frit, stringers, and dichroic glass are all examples of these materials (metal fused to the glass in a vacuum chamber). Fusing temperatures and times for float (window glass) glass are different from those for soda-Lime glass, which has a different COE (coefficient of expansion).

What's the ideal temperature for melting glass?

In the range of 1350 to 1500 degrees Fahrenheit, soda-lime glass will melt and fuse together. Soda-lime glass melts at a temperature 50 degrees higher than float glass does.

Fusing glass at home: is it possible?

It's possible, but only if you have the right kiln and an accurate temperature monitor. Keeping cutting tools and a glass grinder around the house will also come in handy.

Glass fuses in what time period?

It can take anywhere from three to four hours for smaller pieces to up to 13-14 hours for larger ones, depending on the glass and the project's size and thickness. Glass must be cooled to 900–1000 degrees Fahrenheit after fusing to relieve any stress that may have been built up during the firing process.

Ideas for Glass Fusing Beginners

Using fusing glass, you can create a wide range of objects for a wide range of uses. Glass fusing ideas are provided in this article so that you can experiment with new materials and techniques when you next work with glass.

It doesn't take a lot of materials or equipment to make a fusing glass project. Fusible glass, a kiln, and appropriate safety gear are all you need to get started.

In this article, we explain the basics of the art of fusing glass, including what kind of glass you can use, how to do it correctly and what kind of kiln is best based on the pieces you'll be making. Before you start your first project, we recommend reading this article.

CHAPTER THREE

The following are some suggestions for glass fusing projects:

Plates

Fusible glass must be FDA-approved if you plan to use it to make any type of tableware, such as plates or spoons. The label, glass package, or manufacturer's website are the most common places to find this information.

Plates that have been slathered with

Fusible glass strips of different colors are placed on top of each other and melted together in a kiln to create strip plates. You must ensure that the pieces of glass you are working with melt at the same temperature in order for this technique to work properly. If this is not the case, the plate may break once it has cooled.

Using kiln shelves to build a frame, you can get a perfect square or rectangle. Making flat plates or coasters can be a fun way to decorate your home.

Molds, on the other hand, can be used to give them a slight curve, making them more functional.

Strip plate glass fusing designs using this method are shown in the following examples:

Sheet for strip construction in fusing glass

Striped green and red bowl

plate with a kaleidoscope of hues

Plates of the usual variety are available.

Forget about strips if you want something simpler and less time consuming. Glass panels of different colors can be melted together to create simple plates. Here are a few concepts to get you started:

Dichroic glass accents on a purple plate

Glass plate depicting a beach and the ocean that has been fusing

Glass plate with a lime and cobalt fused color

Three types of jewelry: Necklaces, earrings and rings

Fusing glass allows you to make a wide variety of jewelry. Using a variety of fusing techniques, colors, and textures, you can create your own unique glass pendants. Chains and hooks in gold or silver can be used to create fancy necklaces, earrings, and rings, or leather can be used for a more rustic look.

Here are a few concepts:

Necklace made from fused glass and green dichroic

a pendant necklace made from fused glass

Jewellery box made of rustic wood

Earrings in the picasso style of dichroic glass

Drinking straws or "swizzle sticks"

This is one of the simplest glass fusing projects there is. Drinks are stirred with swizzle sticks. The same fusible glass strips that we discussed earlier can be used to make these. Melting a few strips of different colors will do the trick if this is your first project. You can also create multicolor swizzle sticks by building a stick from several small pieces of glass of different colors. Here are a few concepts to get you started:

Red abstract swizzle sticks made of fused glass

Gold-plated cocktail stirrers in clear glass

Drinking swizzle sticks in various colors

Posts for the Yard

Garden stakes made of wood or metal can be used to support newly planted trees, label various plants and flowers, divide your garden into various zones, or simply left as decorative pieces in your front or back yard. Here are a few design concepts to get you started:

Butterfly garden stake made of fused glass

a collection of variously patterned garden stakes

Imaginative garden stakes in cartoon form

Bird stakes for the garden

Ornaments in Glass Fusing for the Holidays

How fun would it be to decorate your Christmas tree with your own handmade ornaments? Well, this year is your year to make it happen!

You'll also need either hooks or metallic cords used for decorating and gift wrapping to hang the ornaments once they're finished.. Candles, bells, birds, wreaths, stars, miniature Christmas trees, Santa Claus, angels, gifts, and candy canes are some of the most popular ornamental elements. Here are a few concepts to get you started:

Christmas gnome in red, white, and green

Toy soldiers made of fused glass

Christmas decorations with glass-fused birds

Assorted Ornaments

With the addition of extra materials, you can transform your pieces into whatever you desire, much like when making Christmas tree ornaments.

You can, for example, purchase small magnets and turn them into fridge magnets, keychains, or wall art by framing your artwork. Ideas for fusing your own glass include:

Fused glass art of cosmic fish

fused-glass trees for the walls

Rainbow-colored fused glass keyring

Fused glass art making supplies

Our glass fusing 101 guide has all the information you need about the supplies, tools, and materials you need to fuse glass if you need help or advice on what to get for your next projects.

You'll need a glass kiln to fuse glass properly. A kiln is a type of oven designed specifically for the drying and melting of ceramics and glass. You can pick from a variety of sizes depending on the final products you want to make.

As an example, microwave kilns typically have a chamber with a diameter of up to 6 inches and work very effectively. Most of them can fuse small pieces of glass in about 10 minutes. If you're only going to be fusing small amounts of glass at a time, this is the most cost-effective option.

An electric glass kiln is by far the best option for those who require more space and plan to fuse glass on a regular basis, whether as a hobby or professionally.

Hope you enjoyed our glass fusing tips. All the best!

THE END